Open Me First

A Tale of the Nativity

An illustrated story by

Marlyne Maynor

Open Me First
A Tale of the Nativity

Author: Marlyne Maynor

Copyright © 2018 Nissi Publishing, Inc.

Nissi Publishing, Inc.
Roanoke, TX

Artwork by Marlyne Maynor.

[1]"No Room." *Night of Miracles*, John W. Peterson, © 1958, Singspiration, Inc., Zondervan Publishing House. All rights reserved.

[2]Shakespeare, *King Henry IV, Part II, Act III, Scene 1*. Public Domain.

Printed in the United States of America.

ISBN: 978-0-944372-30-2

A Word from the Author

For the umpteenth time, I listened to "Carol Of The Bells" being used to get me to buy a new car. I was on the verge of sending my shoe through the TV. I thought, "Why do they have to use the Infant Jesus to sell cars?" Poor Baby Jesus—not much respect there. Words began coming to my mind; so I wrote them down. I wanted to tell the story of Jesus' birth and what Christmas is really supposed to be about. And I wanted to use illlustrations to help people picture what took place.

We humans are infected by the "Saturnalia" virus. I must admit I've suffered this mighty bug myself. Saturnalia was the winter celebration observed by the ancient Romans in honor of the god Saturn. It started around the winter solstice and lasted a week. They exchanged gifts and had parties. It was quite a celebration! When Christianity became Rome's official religion, Saturnalia was merged with Christmas.

People today get so upset if they don't get a new car, cell phone, dental implants or a vacation on the Space Station. It's become all about the gifts, but we already have been given the best gift ever! Remember: "Jesus is the Reason for the Season."

It is my hope that this book will be a blessing to all who read it, and it will accomplish the purpose the Lord wanted when He prompted me to write it.

~ Marlyne

For

Matthew and Luke

who told the story first

He stood silently and gazed at the panorama before Him. Sadly, He observed the horrors of war, the cruel treatment of one human against another, and the corruption of mankind. Soon, He would have to cross the boundary between eternity and time and join that other world. This had all been planned before the foundation of the world.

They had placed their final creation in a wonderful garden in a perfect world. But the two were not satisfied, and it brought disaster and a curse. Ever since then, the descendants of Adam and Eve had been riddled with the curse that couldn't be broken.

God selected a man named Abram to found a great family. Renamed Abraham, he was promised many blessings. Through Abraham's family, all mankind would be blessed. But Abraham's offspring were stubborn and resisted the Lord's way, too. The Lord sent many true and faithful prophets and leaders to bring them back to Him, but they were too obstinate to obey.

The Lord still kept His word that He had made to Abraham. Someone in Abraham's lineage would bring redemption to the fallen family of man.

Beautiful

But Broken

The words of the prophets were coming to pass. Someone was to go into the world as a sacrifice for the sins of all mankind. He would die, but not just any death. He would die the ghastly death of a criminal!

But the best part of this plan was that He would not stay dead but rise to live again. This death would reconcile God and man.

Now the Prince of Peace must lay aside His royal garments and descend to earth. He is to become an embryo in the womb of a Jewish maiden named Mary.

Gabriel, one of the commanders of Heaven's armies, was sent to Galilee with a message for Mary. This young woman was selected from all the other young women of the world. Therefore, she must have been devout and brave. Her father, Joachim, must have given her a strict Jewish upbringing, expecting the fulfillment of long-ago prophecies.

They eagerly waited for Messiah to come!

When Gabriel addressed her one morning, she agreed to be the handmaiden of the Lord. But she had one question. She had no husband, although she was pledged to a carpenter named Joseph. Gabriel explained that this was no human child but a Child by the Holy Spirit. This was a fulfillment of Isaiah's prophecy that a virgin would conceive a Child—a Holy Child.

Mary went to her parents and said,
"Papa, Mama, I have wonderful news ...."

In time, Mary began to feel sick in the mornings, and her body began to change. Mary's family, knowing the story behind her pregnancy, was accepting of the situation.

But Joseph was not. What was he to do? They had not been officially married in a true Jewish celebration ... *and* ... Mary could be stoned to death! And *he* would have to cast the first stone!

Gabriel made another visit—this time in a dream—to Joseph. The angel told Joseph not to be afraid for Mary had conceived a Holy Child—the Messiah. Joseph was supposed to take Mary as his wife and care for her and the Child. Jesus would need a good earthly father, and God had chosen Joseph for that specific purpose, just as He chose Mary to be His mother.

They were very special people.

So Mary and her Joseph were quietly married. The newlyweds settled in and life became as normal as possible. Tongues still wagged, but even this began to cease. Of course, Mary's family was concerned, but her mother was delighted that her very own grandson would be the Anointed One.

Mary became restless with questions. When she heard about her Aunt Elizabeth, she decided to visit her. Elizabeth, who was past childbearing age, found herself pregnant. Her husband, a Temple priest, had also been visited by an angel. Zacharias, also quite elderly, didn't believe the angel's news that he was going to be a father! But his child would be the forerunner of the Messiah. He would be great in the sight of the Lord, and he was to be named John. So Zacharias, because of his unbelief, was struck dumb until little John was born.

When the women saw each other, silver-haired Elizabeth and Mary, just in her teens, Elizabeth's baby leapt for joy in her womb. The women had much to talk about.

"Blessed are you among women,
and blessed is the fruit of your womb."

Luke 1:42 (NKJV)

Mary stayed with Elizabeth for three months. Then the time for Elizabeth to give birth had come. It was unseemly for Mary to be present, so she traveled back to Galilee.

When Elizabeth's time came, she delivered her son. Her neighbors and relatives heard how the Lord had shown mercy to her, and they rejoiced with her. When Zacharias and Elizabeth took the baby to the temple and Zacharias wrote that his name would be John, he was able to speak again and began to praise God and prophesy over his son.

"You, my child, will be called
a prophet of the Most High;
for you will go on before the Lord
to prepare the way for Him,
to give His people the knowledge of salvation
through the forgiveness of their sins."

Luke 1:76–77 (NIV)

Another trial was on the horizon for Mary and Joseph. Caesar Augustus, needing money for his rich lifestyle and extensive wars, issued a proclamation for taxation. Every man was to return to the place of his birth to register for the taxation. This came at the time Mary's baby was due, but they had no choice. Of course, Mary's mother wanted her to stay with them while Joseph was gone, but much to her dismay, Mary decided she needed to go with Joseph.

This would mean a journey of four or five days—a 90-mile walk! They had a small donkey so Mary could ride if she needed to. Not much comfort for Mary at all.

Both Mary and Joseph were descended from King David—Royal, but poor. Joseph had descended through Solomon's bloodline; Mary's royal ancestor was Nathan.

The trip was uneventful, but meeting other kinsmen was an adventure. They slept on the road under a dazzling display of stars.

Before they reached Bethlehem, for that was their destination, Mary went into labor. At first, she encountered little twinges of pain, but soon it became gripping labor.

When they arrived, the sun was setting. The town was full of pilgrims seeking shelter for the night. David's city was full of his offspring in need of a bed and a good meal. Joseph searched desperately for a place for his laboring wife, but there was no room for them at the inn.

The inn was even perhaps a large community room with space only for bedrolls. No privacy there!

"No room, only a manger of hay,
No room, He is a stranger today,
No room, here in His world
turned away. No room." [1]

The innkeeper remembered the space out back where the animals were housed. It would at least be warm and dry without prying eyes to look on Mary in her labor. So Mary and Joseph took refuge among the birds and livestock. There, Mary gave birth to the long-awaited Savior of the world.

Did Mary have assistance and the comfort of another woman or did Joseph serve as midwife to her? It was not customary for a man to be present during childbirth.

Regardless, the King of kings and Lord of lords was born into the world in a place where there was the sound of animals, the smell of the barnyard and perhaps the chill of the night. No angel came down from Heaven to deliver Mary's Child. Rather, it was just as every birth had been since the beginning. The Infant, in addition to being Son of God was Son of Man also. He was like man. He was man.

Mary Meets Her Savior

So He came not as a conquering hero on a milky white horse with a Heavenly army following Him. He came as a red and wrinkled, squalling bit of the human race.

Mary, with foresight, had packed baby things just in case. After she had nursed Him and dressed Him, she needed a place to lay Him down to sleep. There was no cradle, so they had to make do with a feeding trough the animals used. Joseph put clean, fresh hay in for their son, whom they called Jesus, as the angel had instructed them to do.

The day had been exhausting, but Joseph had done admirably for his little family, and he laid down to sleep on a pile of hay. As Mary studied her newborn son, she counted His fingers and toes and admired the perfection of her darling. She, too, after spending a little time with Him, went to sleep.

But they were about to have visitors.

One of the chief occupations of Bethlehem was raising sheep—not a pleasant job, for sheep are smelly and not very bright. Bethlehem is almost six miles from the great city of Jerusalem. Long ago, the prophet Micah had foreseen that Bethlehem would be the place for the Messiah's birth.

Interestingly, the flocks of Bethlehem supplied the sacrificial lambs for the Temple in Jerusalem.

Interesting that the Lamb of God would be delivered where those very lambs were born and raised.

The night sky was a riotous display of glory, just as it had been since God made the stars to shine. The stars seemed so close you could almost catch a handful of them! The flocks were quiet and sleeping, but the shepherds had to be watchful for nighttime thieves.

Then the sky changed! A form detached
itself from the brilliant light declaring:

"Fear not!"

It was a mighty angel who had come from the
Throne of God to announce the glad tidings.
The long-awaited Messiah had been born
and was sleeping in a manger! Suddenly,
the sky opened and a great multitude of the
heavenly hosts were singing:

"Glory to God!"

and

"Peace on Earth."

Then the sky returned to normal once again.
The shepherds left their flocks and hurried
into town to see the miracle for themselves.

A week passed quickly, and soon, Baby Jesus was eight days old. Since His birth, Mary had changed Him, fed Him, and watched Him grow. She loved Him more and more every day. Sometimes, she even forgot He was the Son of God and saw Him as just her precious baby. She watched carefully to see some new thing He had accomplished. Was He recognizing her and Joseph yet? He was surely the smartest, most beautiful and best baby ever (all new moms think that).

And He was.

Someone has said that time is not a friend to mothers. Soon that tiny being would be a crawling baby, an adventurous toddler, and then a young person leaving his home. The only place that tiny baby would live would be in his mother's memory.

So Mary treasured this time with her Son.

But now was the time for His circumcision. Was Mary happy about that? Surely not; she didn't want pain inflicted on her darling. But circumcision was a sign of God's covenant with Abraham. All Jewish boys had it done, so Jesus would undergo it, too.

While at the Temple, they met a very old man named Simeon. God had promised him he would not die before he saw the Consolation of Israel. He recognized Baby Jesus as The One. He took the Baby in his arms and blessed Him. Now he was ready to die. He told Mary that because of this Child, her heart would cleave in two. These were dire warnings for the young couple.

There was also an elderly widow named Anna who devoted her entire existence to God, serving Him in the Temple with fasting and prayers night and day. She also recognized the Baby was the Messiah and took Him in her arms and blessed Him.

"My eyes have seen your salvation."

Luke 2:30 (NKJV)

In the next few months, they were able to find a small house where they could take care of each other and the growing Baby. A carpenter could always find work.

One day as Joseph was working in his shop and Mary was busy with her endless chores, there was a loud commotion at their door. Mary was surprised to see what amounted to be a small caravan. Some of the men were richly dressed while others looked like servants or animal trainers.

Several of the men approached the door, bowing very reverently to her. They inquired as to where they could find the young Child. They were wise men from the East who studied the stars. They knew of the Promised Messiah from the stories told by the Jewish captives living in Persia some centuries before. They had seen a great star arise, and they had followed it to find and worship the King of the Jews. Then they presented their gifts to Him—gold, frankincense, and myrrh.

Before coming to Bethlehem; however, they had stopped to inquire at Herod's palace. They presumed the little King would be in the palace. Herod was one of the most evil men who had ever lived. He was insanely jealous for his throne. Many had died because of this including a wife and two sons.

Herod, conniving fox that he was, pretended that he, too, wanted to find the Child—to worship Him. He wanted the Magi to come back after they had found Him and tell him where He was. After seeing Baby Jesus, their mission was complete. They wanted to return home. They had a dream in which they were told not to go back to Herod but to follow a different route than what they had used.

"Uneasy lies the head
that wears the crown."

Shakespeare[2]

An angel also appeared to Joseph in a dream. He was to take Mary and the young Child and flee to Egypt because Herod would seek the Child to destroy Him.

Meanwhile, Herod became irate when he realized the Magi were not going to come tell him where the Child was. He stormed about seeking a way to destroy this new menace to his throne. After all, the "Wise Men" had called the Child the "King of the Jews."

So this madman ordered his soldiers to go into Bethlehem and slay all the baby boys who were two years of age and under.

Thus he earned for himself the name of the Butcher of Bethlehem. There was much sorrow in Bethlehem which fulfilled the prophecy in Jeremiah of "Rachel weeping for her children, refusing to be comforted because they are no more (Jeremiah 31:15, NKJV)."

Mary, Joseph and Jesus traveled to Egypt where they dwelled until Herod had died and an angel told Joseph in a dream once again that he could return to Israel for those who had sought to kill the Child were dead. And another prophecy was fulfilled from Hosea that said, "Out of Egypt I called My Son (Hosea 11:1 NIV)."

Joseph took them to live in Nazareth. There he set up his carpenter shop and Jesus learned his trade. Their family increased as Mary had more children.

He grew in wisdom, stature, and favor with God and man and became known as Jesus of Nazareth.

"Out of Egypt
I called My Son."

At 30 years of age, Jesus began His earthly ministry. He preached, taught, healed, and raised the dead. He also raised the ire of the religious leaders of Israel with His radical views of Jehovah as a loving Father. It ended when they conducted a false trial and had Him crucified. He rose from the tomb on the third day, just as He told His followers He would. After further instructions and a promise to return, He ascended to Heaven. His gospel has spread over the world with millions of followers over the centuries.

An epilogue cannot be written because as Gabriel said to Mary, "There will be no end of His kingdom."

Jesus Christ was known by many names—The King of Kings, the Lord of Lords and many more. He was called The Lion of Judah which points to His claim to the throne through David and His ancestor, Judah, who was a mighty conquering monarch. The Lamb of God is His name which represents His sacrifice and meek obedience to His Father.

Combined, these two names give a picture of a mighty ruler, but tender and kind. Together, they make a picture of the future age when the animals will all lie down together in peace.

www.ingramcontent.com/pod-product-compliance
Lightning Source LLC
Chambersburg PA
CBHW041634040426
42447CB00020B/3486